Cat's Got Your Tongue

Cat's Got Your Tongue

A Book of Riddles

Richard McMenamin, Shari McMenamin, and Michele Van Troba
Illustrations by Albert Van Troba

Ten Speed Press
Berkeley, California

This book's concept, artwork, and finished product is dedicated to Richard E. McMenamin—the "Big Mac" in the hearts of his son, daughter, and their respective and respectful spouses.

Ten Speed Press
P.O. Box 7123
Berkeley, California 94707
www.tenspeed.com

Distributed in Australia by Simon and Schuster Australia, in Canada by Ten Speed Press Canada, in New Zealand by Southern Publishers Group, in South Africa by Real Books, in Southeast Asia by Berkeley Books, and in the United Kingdom and Europe by Airlift Books.

Design by Lisa Patrizio
Illustrations by Albert Van Troba

Library of Congress Cataloging-in-Publication Data

McMenamin, Richard.
    Cat's got your tongue / verse by Richard McMenamin, Shari McMenamin and Michele van Troba; Illustrations by Albert van Troba.
      p. cm.
    ISBN 1-58008-066-9
    1. Cats—Humor.   2. Puns and punning.   3. Riddles.   I. McMenamin, Shari.
II. Troba, michele van. III. Troba, Albert van. IV. Title.
PN6231.C23M39 1999
818'.5402—dc21   98-54973
                               CIP

First printing, 1999

PRINTED IN HONG KONG

1 2 3 4 5 6 7 8 9 10 — 03 02 01 00 99

Contents

Introduction

The Riddle

Tyger! Tyger! burning bright
In the forests of the night,
What immortal hand or eye
Could frame thy fearful symmetry?

Blake pondered the mystery and so do we.

Why do we love our cats? They have free access to our homes and our affections. They are family. We talk to them, and they talk back.

Cats were the first animals to be domesticated. Or were we caticated? Sometimes we wonder. The ancient Egyptians worshipped them and built monuments to them, too: "The Riddle of the Sphinx." Was this because of the cats' mystical natures or on the basis of their hunting prowess in protecting the great Egyptian graineries from thieving mice and other critters?

Throughout the ages cats have been purrsecuted as the familiars of witches. No kitting, cats were burned at the stake during the Inquisition and at the Salem witch trials.

What makes our cats unique? What sets them apart? What makes them purrfect? In essence, that is exactly it—their ability to purr. This is the innate magic of cats: the soothing music they play for us as they sit upon our laps. No other animal can mimic a purr or give us the tranquility and love conveyed by this harmonic communication.

Cat's Got Your Tongue

This book had its genesis in our relationships with our cats. What if they could talk? What if the roles were reversed? We began to realize how prevalent the word cat was in our language.

The riddle deepened. As in the Shakespearean script, we began to see the "play within a play" or the "word within a word." Cat was everywhere and held a "meaning within a meaning." The English language was caticized. Not only directly but phonetically.

What developed was not only a word riddle, but almost magically, for each word, an entire scene. These scenes were captured by our artist in original oil paintings. The scenes, initially a reaction to the riddle, have taken on a life of their own and stand alone. The paw of fate was at work.

How to Play

The rules are simple. Guess the word. The answer will either directly or phonetically contain the word cat. Some are easy, some are tough. One requires a genius.

The most important rule is to have fun! We hope you catch on.

EXAMPLE

Question: What do you call the process that the Egyptians used to tame Great Grandpa Pharo McCat?

Clue: The answer to this riddle
Is how they made Grandpa civil.

Answer: Domestication

How We Got Published

(The final riddle)

For those of you who do not yet believe in the mystical qualities of cats, we have a true story for you. Once this book was complete, for several days we discussed how to get it published. We did not know where to start. Our two cats, Samantha and Rae, shared our concern.

For three days in a row, they sat kitty-corner from our worktable, just inside the back door where we keep our bikes, and meowed. We thought it strange that they were sitting on the bike seats and caterwauling, something that they had never done before. We solved the riddle and got the greatest publishers in the world. You guessed it, they were sitting on our *ten-speeds*.

The Characters

This book is about two families of cats, the McCats and the Van Cats. If one notes the authors' names, it will be clear where the eponymic roots of our two cat families lie.

The McCats and Van Cats live in the city of Catalonia. The McCats are a clean-living, hardworking clan. They may have a wee drop on a special occasion, but their vices are few.

The Van Cats on the other hand are, to be kind, from the wrong side of the tracks. They don't care for working, but they like money—a bad combination. However, they are reformable. Some are good-hearted—and even become artists.

Categories

Home Life

The first scenes introduce us to the nuclear McCat family. We begin by eating dinner with the McCats. We visit Mama and Father McCat's job sites. The children take us to their rooms, athletic events, and play.

Religious Life

The McCats are traditionalists and are strongly religious. We go to church with the McCats, pay respect to their ancestors, and attend parochial class with Bobby and Susie.

The Elder McCats

Grandpa and Grandma McCat are elderly and face the problems of senior citizens. We go to the hospital with Grandpa and then spend an afternoon with him sharing his favorite pastime. Grandma is sweet but in the dark to many things.

Uncle Cheshire McCat

Of course Uncle Cheshire is smiling. He has lived the American dream. From lowly beginnings, he has climbed to the top. We follow Uncle Cheshire's rise to fame from the prairies of Texas through the oil fields to the world of the rich and famous.

The Van Cats

The Van Cats provide the duality necessary to balance the McCats' goodness. Tom Van Cat tries to make it in polite society but backslides on occasion. He is partial to strong drink, which leads him to follow his animal instincts, much to his ultimate chagrin.

Dick Van Cat presents us with the greatest metamorphosis in the book. We find him as a common criminal of the streets. He receives the punishment of society but escapes. He not only escapes his temporal bonds but also finds transcendence of heart. One might say he makes the antihero's journey. However, he still cannot answer the riddle that has plagued the cat world since the beginning of time: Why is *God* spelled backwards *dog?*

Aunt Wanda is uniquely gifted for her profession and is a character who certainly opens the door to further exploration. She whips up the imagination. Uncle Joe is a blue-collar beer-drinking good ole boy. He likes to fish and his physical appearance is the cartography of his life.

The McCats' Special Occasions

In the final scenes, we follow the McCats through their summer camping trip. They love to spend time together. The McCats stick together and weather the storm.

Finally we share the Christmas season with the McCats, as they experience the excitement of gifts and the relaxation of an evening in their living room gathered around the fireplace.

The Family Tree

McCats

Van Cats

GRANDPA
Michael
McCat

GRANDMA
Tomasina
O'Cat

GRANDPA
Black Bart
Van Cat

GRANDMA
Madame
Cat

UNCLE
Cheshire
McCat

FATHER
Romeo
McCat

MOTHER
Juliet
Van Cat

AUNT
Wanda
Van Cat

UNCLE
Joe
Van Cat

UNCLE
Tom
Van Cat

AUNT
Kate
Van Cat

SISTER
Susie
McCat

BROTHER
Bobby
McCat

COUSIN
Dick
Van Cat

WHAT IS THE McCAT FAMILY'S FAVORITE MEAL?

When the McCats want a treat,
They catch this in the creek.

Catfish

WHAT DO THE McCATS PUT ON THEIR CATFISH?

Upon their fish they place this paste
To enhance taste.

Catsup

WHAT IS MOTHER McCAT'S BUSINESS?

When Mama McCat kneads some dough,
Where does she go?

Catering

WHAT DOES FATHER McCAT DRIVE FOR A LIVING?

Father McCat is a hardworking man.
He uses this machine to level the land.

Caterpillar

WHAT POSITION DOES BOBBY McCAT PLAY ON THE BASEBALL TEAM?

Bobby wears a mask,
To do this task.

Catcher

WHERE DOES BOBBY McCAT LIKE TO BE WHEN HE IS UP TO BAT?

This count makes Bobby smile
Before he hits the ball a mile.

Catbird Seat

WHAT IS SUSIE McCAT'S FAVORITE GAME?

Susie sits upon her bed
And spins this web.

Cat's Cradle

WHAT DID THE KIDS CALL SUSIE McCAT WHEN SHE WAS AFRAID TO COME DOWN FROM THE TREE?

When timid Susie is not being brave,
They call her this because she is afraid.

Scaredy-Cat

WHERE DO THE McCATS GO TO CHURCH ON SUNDAY?

In following their vocation,
The McCats head to this location.

Cathedral

WHERE DO THE McCATS PAY THEIR LAST RESPECTS?

This is not for the McCats' hair.
It is a place for respectful prayer.

Catacombs

WHAT RELIGION ARE THE McCATS?

In this age of many denominations,
This is the McCats' congregation.

Catholic

WHAT DO THE McCAT CHILDREN STUDY AT SCHOOL?

When Bobby and Susie go to school,
This is a source for the Golden Rule.

Catechism

THE POLICE TEACH THE McCAT CHILDREN TO "JUST SAY NO" TO THIS.

In this day of drug abuse,
Bobby and Susie are taught not to use.

Catnip

GRANDPA McCAT UNDERWENT
A SPECIAL TEST AT THE HOSPITAL.

It used to be called an X ray.
Now three-dimensional is the only way.

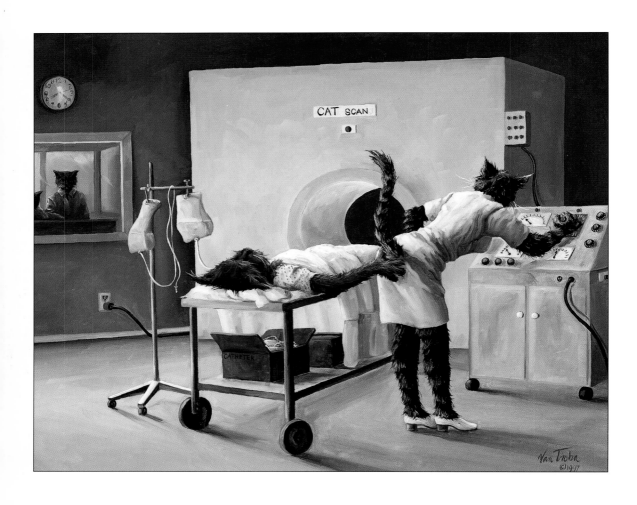

CAT Scan

WHAT IS WRONG WITH GRANDMA McCAT'S EYES?

Grandma McCat is so kind
It's terrible these almost made her blind.

Cataracts

WHAT DOES GRANDPA McCAT ENJOY EVERY AFTERNOON?

At midday Grandpa always thinks
That he needs these forty winks.

Catnap

WHAT DOES UNCLE CHESHIRE McCAT DRIVE?

Uncle Cheshire smokes a big cigar
And drives this luxury car.

Cadillac

WHAT WAS UNCLE CHESHIRE McCAT'S FIRST BUSINESS?

The pies that these make
Mother McCat doesn't bake.

Cattle

HOW DID UNCLE CHESHIRE McCAT MAKE HIS FORTUNE?

The goal of this "boring toil"
Is a gusher of black oil.

Wildcatting

WHERE DOES UNCLE CHESHIRE McCAT LIKE TO VACATION?

For sailors this island is a blessing.
You can also use it as a salad dressing.

Catalina

WHO DOES UNCLE CHESHIRE McCAT ASSOCIATE WITH?

To be a member of this lifestyle,
You must be wealthy or have a title.

Aristocats

WHO IS UNCLE CHESHIRE McCAT'S GIRLFRIEND?

Uncle Cheshire has a discerning mind.
He picked her as his favorite feline.

Cat's Meow

WHAT DOES MISS CAT'S MEOW HEAR WHEN SHE WALKS DOWN THE STREET?

Cat's Meow is such a flirt,
She can't avoid this in her short skirt.

Catcalls

WHAT IS BOBBY McCAT'S PART-TIME JOB FOR UNCLE CHESHIRE McCAT?

When Bobby's bank account gets low,
He takes his uncle's clubs in tow.

Caddy

WHAT IS UNCLE TOM VAN CAT'S
FAVORITE COCKTAIL?

When Uncle Tom feels he can't win
He has a cup of this sin.

Gin and Catatonic

WHERE DOES UNCLE TOM VAN CAT GO WHEN THE BAR IS CLOSED?

This is a house of ill repute.
That Uncle Tom shouldn't be here is not in dispute.

Cathouse

WHAT HAPPENS WHEN AUNT KATE VAN CAT TRACKS HIM DOWN?

Late at night you hear this out your window.
It's just Aunt Kate collecting her sinful.

Catfight

WHO LED COUSIN DICK VAN CAT ASTRAY?

On lighted streets these cats find no rest.
It's dark byways they like the best.

Alley Cats

HOW DOES COUSIN DICK VAN CAT GET MONEY?

He comes at night, so be aware.
He cleans out your house, even silverware.

Cat Burglar

WHERE DID COUSIN DICK VAN CAT GET BUSTED?

It's used to get from here to there.
This ambulating takes place high in the air.

Catwalk

WHERE DID THEY SEND
COUSIN DICK VAN CAT?

A life of crime was the reason
Cousin Dick ended up in this famous prison.

Alcatraz

HOW DID COUSIN
DICK VAN CAT ESCAPE?

It's really nothing but a lever,
And Cousin Dick was very clever.

Catapult

HOW DID HE END UP?

Cousin Dick met defeat.
This time he didn't land on his feet.

Catawampus

WHO PUT COUSIN DICK VAN CAT ON THE RIGHT TRACK?

This man of the cloth
Ended Cousin Dick's life of sloth.

Catalytic Converter

WHAT DID COUSIN DICK VAN CAT EXPERIENCE AT HIS BAPTISM?

When Cousin Dick was redeemed,
His soul was cleaned.

Catharsis

WHY DOES EVERYONE TAKE COVER WHEN WICKED AUNT WANDA VAN CAT COMES TO VISIT?

She creates havoc with one flip
Of this ancient whip.

Cat-o'-Nine-Tails

WHAT DOES TOUGH OLD UNCLE JOE VAN CAT USE FOR FISHING?

Uncle Joe uses this for fishin'.
It could also be used by a physician.

Catgut

WHAT DOES THE McCAT FAMILY TAKE IN THE SUMMER?

The McCats used the bathroom and packed the car,
But Mama remembered the hot iron before too far.

Vacation

THE McCAT FAMILY ENJOYS
SAILING ON A . . .

The McCats' boat is split in two.
This helps to stabilize you.
(The Hawaiians used it, too.)

Catamaran

WHAT GETS TOLD AROUND THE McCATS' CAMPFIRE?

Father McCat tells this after some ale.
They also grow in the marshy swale.

Cattails

WHAT HAPPENS WHEN THE TORNADO HITS THE McCAT CAMP?

Hurricane, fire, and flood—
The Red Cross will be there to give blood.

Catastrophe

HOW DO THE McCAT CHILDREN GET SANTA CLAUS GOING AT CHRISTMAS TIME?

Bobby and Susie check this over.
They want to be sure and get their Christmas trover.

Catalyst

WHAT DOES THE McCAT FAMILY BURN IN THEIR FIREPLACE?

When the shopping is done
and the presents are wrapped,
The McCats burn these for the warm winter's nap.

Catalogs

WHAT IS OUR ARTIST'S FAVORITE PASTIME?

Our poor artist can hardly keep up the pace
Because he loves drawing his own face.

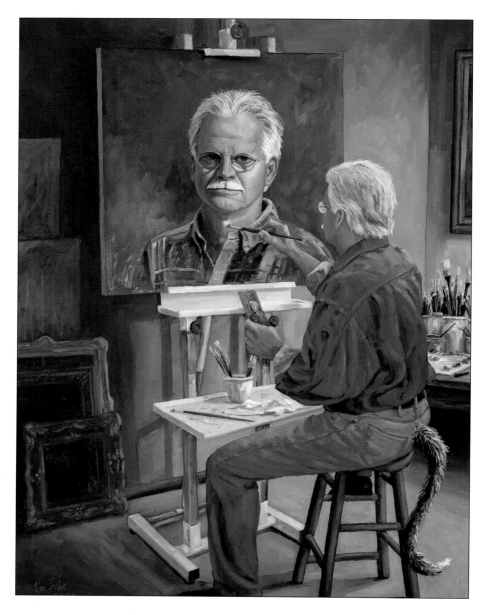

Caricatures

About the Authors

The McMenamins

The creative genius behind this book is Richard McMenamin, World Famous Attorney, C.P.A., author, sportsman, etc. He is not only good looking, but smart too! His achievements are surpassed only by his humility. Rich lives on the shores of Lake Crescent, Washington, in the isolated Olympic Peninsula. He spends his time in the solitude of the virgin forests anticipating his transcendence.

Shari and Rich McMenamin met at college in 1972. Rich was thunder-struck and they have been together ever since. They attended law school together and are currently partners in the law firm of McMenamin & McMenamin. Until recently their two cats, Rae and Samantha, constituted their family. That changed on September 2, 1998, with the birth of their first child (a gift from God), Alexandria.

The McMenamins live in the heart of the Olympic National Park. The king of cats, the cougar, calls their backyard home.

The Van Trobas

Albert and Michele Van Trobas's love story began when they first met at the high school where they taught; it continues to this day. Albert has been an art instructor for thirty years. In his youth, he was a world-class miler, running against the likes of Jim Ryan. Michele keeps Al running still. Al is fully dedicated to his art, which includes a sweeping portfolio of wildlife landscapes, carica-tures, and creatively enhanced portraits.

Michele is currently a substitute teacher, busy mother, homemaker, and projects coordinator.

The Van Trobas live on Puget Sound. Their daughter, Aubrey, and yellow Lab, Buck, play in the waves in their front yard.

There are many cat lovers and art lovers, too. We had a lot of fun with this book and hope you do as well. Creating the illustrations took a lot of time and work. Each was painstakingly created in original oils, then reproduced for publication through advanced technological methods that captured the originals in full detail.

The actual McCat and Van Cat paintings will be available in limited edition prints. For additional information, contact:

McMenamin & McMenamin
306 E. Eighth St.
Port Angeles, WA 98362
(360) 452-2793